Standing Bear of the Ponca

Virginia Driving Hawk Sneve

Illustrated by Thomas Floyd

University of Nebraska Press
Lincoln and London

Library of Congress Cataloging-in-Publication Data

Sneve, Virginia Driving Hawk.

Standing Bear of the Ponca / Virginia Driving Hawk Sneve; illustrated by Thomas Floyd.

pages cm.

Includes bibliographical references.

ISBN 978-0-8032-2826-9 (pbk.: alk. paper) 1. Standing Bear, Ponca chief—Juvenile literature.
2. Ponca Indians—Kings and rulers—Biography—Juvenile literature. 3. Ponca Indians—
Relocation—Juvenile literature. 4. Ponca Indians—Claims—Juvenile literature.
I. Floyd, Thomas L., illustrator. II. Title.

E99.P7S836 2013

978.004'9752440092–dc23

[B]   2013004407

Set in Sabon Next LT Pro by J. Vadnais.

Designed by J. Vadnais.

Contents

Introduction

"I am a man," Standing Bear told a crowded Omaha courtroom. Then he declared that his blood was the same color as that of any person in the room.

He made those claims at the end of a famous trial. That court case showed that an American Indian had the same rights as any other person in the United States.

Standing Bear was not the main leader of the Ponca tribe. He was a chief of the Bear Clan. As such, he was responsible for taking care of one small band. His bold acts to care for his family and followers made him famous in Nebraska and all across the country.

As a result, many white people began to support American Indian causes. Other Indians noted what Standing Bear had done too. They were encouraged to fight for their own rights. The Standing Bear trial was historic. For the first time, the law said that "an Indian is a person under the law"—a person who has rights just like any other American.

Standing Bear, the Boy

It was always a good day for the Ponca when a child was born. The tribe treasured its children. But when the chief's son was born, he was doubly welcomed. One day this boy would be the head of the Bear Clan. He would be a leader and take care of his people.

The mother took the baby's umbilical cord. She put it into an amulet bag. That was a leather pouch shaped like a horned toad. The toad was a symbol of long life and endurance. The parents did not know their son would face many troubles in his life, but they believed the amulet had powers to protect him. For all of his life that bag was kept in a special place in the lodge.

The boy's mother sang soothing songs to quiet and lull him to sleep. He was with her all day in a cradleboard on her back. Sometimes she set it nearby or hung it from a tree. There the baby watched her at her work. He could also see the things going on in the village.

Children were not allowed outdoors at night. Their mothers warned them that there was a monster outside, so they'd better be good and go to bed.

The boy grew older. When he did something bad, he was gently scolded. He was never spanked. The Ponca believed that hitting a child would hurt the child's spirit.

The boy was trained to respect the old ones. He was never to walk in front of a seated person without permission. He was taught to say thank you. He learned to play quietly and to speak softly around adults. He knew that it was improper to stare at strangers.

When he could walk by himself, the boy was considered a person. He was no longer a baby. It was time for the ceremony of "Turning the Child." He stood on a stone in the center of the family's lodge. An elder turned him to each of the four directions. The elder cut a lock of the boy's hair and then gave him a new pair of moccasins. Then the boy was given his new grown-up name.

He was now Ma-ch-nah-zha, Standing Bear.

Standing Bear was the eldest son in the family. He was treated like a special child. But he also had duties in his home. He helped take care of his younger brother, Big Snake.

In those days Ponca children did not go to school to study in classrooms. Girls learned from their mothers and other women. Boys learned from their fathers and other men. They also spent a lot of time with grandparents. The elders had time to tell stories. One tale was about a yellow-haired beast that lived in a cave above the river. They also told stories of little men who protected a special hill on the plains.

Standing Bear's and Big Snake's grandparents did other things for them too. Their grandmother would have sewn their first ceremonial clothing. Their grandfather would have made their first bows and arrows.

Boys played at war. They used red hay stems as arrows. They snapped the heads of flowers at each other. They learned how grown men should act by watching the respected men of the tribe.

The boys cared for the horse herd near the village. A strong youngster helped break in a horse by riding it in three feet of water. The horse could not buck in the slippery mud. If the boy fell off, he was not hurt in the shallow water.

When a boy was old enough, he became interested in girls. Then he began braiding his hair. When he wanted to marry, he asked his parents to help him. If they liked the girl he had chosen, he could take a horse or buffalo robe to her family. If her parents liked the young man, they kept the gift. Then the couple could marry.

In their early teens, boys went on Vision Quests. They did that to receive spiritual power. A boy would go by himself to a high hill. He would fast—or go without eating—and pray for four days and nights. A bird or animal would visit him. The animal would give him power to help him in his life.

When the boy came down from the hill, he made a small leather sack. This was called a medicine bag. The boy would put an item in the bag—maybe a feather or a claw. It was to remind him of the creature that had given him power. Later as a man, he could gain more power by doing the Sun Dance.

The Tribe

The Sun Dance was held in midsummer. It was the Ponca's most sacred ceremony. Like the Vision Quest, it lasted four days and nights. The dancers had no sleep, no food, and no water. While they danced, they looked at the Thunderbird's (eagle's) nest high on a center pole. At the same time, they blew on an eagle-bone whistle. The men felt they were closer to Wakanda, or the Great Spirit, as they circled the pole.

The Sun Dance was a hard ritual for the men to perform. But they did it because they believed the dance would bring rain for the crops and grass for the buffalo. The men who finished the dance became members of the Soldier Lodge Society. Only the bravest men could join and gain more spiritual power.

Standing Bear had great power, which led him to become a leader at an early age. He became chief of the Bear Clan, so he was responsible for it and had to make sure the tribe's ceremonies were properly done. Once a thunderstorm threatened to end a sacred dance. Standing Bear rose to face the storm and made a powerful prayer, and the storm went away.

There was power in the Ponca's homeland on the river. "Running Water" was the Ponca name for the Niobrara. Above it gentle hills sloped down to green bottomlands. There the Niobrara flowed into the Missouri River. White chalk bluffs towered above the meeting of waters. The Ponca burial ground was on one of those bluffs.

The Ponca said they saw a water monster in the rivers. It may have been what is known today as a paddlefish. Their ancient stories also tell of a hairy elephant on the bluffs. This might have been a woolly mammoth.

The Ponca had once been a part of the Omaha, Osage, Quapaw, and Kansa tribes. They had migrated from the Atlantic coast before 1500. Later the Ponca and Omaha separated from the others and settled in what would become Nebraska. The Ponca stayed at the Niobrara site while the Omaha moved further south.

The Ponca lived in houses made out of earth. Each house was shaped like an igloo. Near their homes on the good lands by the river, they planted corn, squash, pumpkins, beans, and tobacco. The crops grew well in cool spring rains and long, warm summers. After the plants were tall, all the people in the village would leave for a summer buffalo hunt. They would travel as far west as the Black Hills. In the fall they would return to harvest the crops.

The Ponca had a special way to line up for the hunting trip. A beautiful horse went first. This gentle beast carried the tribe's holy pipe inside a sacred bundle. The pipe keeper rode alongside. The hunt leader came next and then all of the hunters. The women and children followed with the camp supplies.

A man who was a brave warrior and a good hunter led the hunt. Other men were chosen as buffalo police. They kept eager hunters from spooking a herd until all was ready.

A successful hunt was important because the dried buffalo meat was the tribe's winter food. Bones were made into tools. Furry hides made warm beds and blankets. Many hides were sewn together to make teepees.

The Ponca had gotten horses from the Comanche in the mid-1700s. They were soon skilled horsemen. Young boys went hunting with the men. Their duty was to take care of the packhorses. Some of them went with the scouts to look for buffalo. When a herd was spotted, the boys ran to alert the main hunting party.

Brave Ponca warriors also protected their families from raids by the Sioux and Pawnee. Boys about twelve or thirteen years old went on war parties. They did not fight but helped by getting water and firewood for the camp. They watched the men fight and listened to battle stories.

Over time the boys saw more and more white men come up the river. These were fur traders who knew the tribe as a peaceful and friendly people. The Ponca were proud that none of them had ever killed a white man.

The white traders also brought smallpox. That disease killed half of the tribe. In 1804 there were only about two hundred Ponca left.

3

Change

The Ponca survived the smallpox, but their way of life was changing. The U.S. government began to control their lives. In 1817 and 1825 the Ponca signed treaties with the government. In those treaties the tribe agreed to give up some of its land and to remain peaceful. In return the government promised to protect the Ponca.

Then the Ponca began to live much like white people. Other whites moved near them on land the Ponca had given up in the treaties.

Standing Bear wore white man's clothes.

He built a log house, a stable, a cattle shed, and a pigpen. He farmed with oxen and plows. He used pitchforks, shovels, and other farming tools. His fourteen-year-old son, Bear Shield, helped with the chores.

Standing Bear had more than one Ponca wife. This was the practice among warrior/hunter tribes where there were more women than men. His first wife died after bearing him two daughters. He then married Susette and her niece Lottie. Susette was the mother of Bear Shield.

The Ponca signed more treaties with the

U.S. government. In each one the Ponca gave up more land. In return, the government promised to help them farm and to educate their children. The government would also protect the tribe.

But the government did not keep its promises. Life was not easy for the Ponca. There were more Sioux raids. The Ponca had to defend themselves. Standing Bear reported the problem to the government agent, A. J. Carrier. Standing Bear said, "When I go to my field, I have got to go with my rifle on my back, and when I work, I must keep one eye on my plow and one eye on those hills yonder."

The Sioux often raced their ponies down from the hills to attack the Ponca village.

Now the weather began to change. The rain did not fall, and the corn wilted without water. Millions of grasshoppers ate what little was left of the crop. The Ponca were in danger of starving.

Then in 1868 the U.S. government signed a treaty with the tribes. It set up a large reservation for them that included most of what later became South Dakota, west of the Missouri River. But a mistake had been made. The Ponca land now belonged to the Sioux.

The Sioux wanted the Ponca off their land. They called the Ponca "women" because they lived like farmers. In the Sioux tribe only women planted crops.

The Sioux ran through the Ponca fields and pulled the corn from the ground. They tore apart the earth houses and destroyed them. Time after time the Ponca rebuilt the lodges, but the Sioux ruined them too many times. Then the Ponca had to live in teepees.

In 1873 more than two hundred Sioux warriors attacked the Ponca. One band came from the bluffs; another came from the river. This time the Ponca were able to drive the enemy away.

The Ponca could not hunt buffalo because of the Sioux raids. The government did not help protect them. Still they tried to be peaceful. At the Agency, they built a church. Many of them attended services every Sunday. Up to seventy-five children went to the Agency school. But life was getting harder for Standing Bear and his people.

The government would not help the Ponca, but the Omaha did. In 1873 the Omaha agreed to sell part of their reservation to the Ponca. Although the Ponca did not want to leave their home on the Niobrara, they agreed to move, to be safe from the Sioux raids. But that did not happen.

Two years later the Ponca met with Mr. Carrier, their agent. They thought he had approved their move to Omaha land. But the agent thought the Ponca had agreed to move much further south.

4

Indian Territory

The Ponca tried to live like the white men. They sent their children to school to learn to read and write English. Knowing how to use the white man's language would help them when they grew up.

The children went to church with their parents. They helped them understand the minister's words. The Ponca could not believe what he told them in the fall of 1876. He said they would soon have to leave their homes and go further south. They had to move to Indian Territory in Oklahoma. It was land set aside for Indians from all over the United States.

The minister said he was sorry for the Ponca, but he could not help them. The Ponca had to move to Oklahoma.

The Ponca were upset and had many questions. Still nothing happened until January 1877. Then a man named E. C. Kemble came to the Agency. He was a U.S. tribal inspector. He called a meeting in the church.

White Eagle, the head chief of all the Ponca, asked where the new land was located. Kemble told him it was six hundred miles to the south.

White Eagle shook his head "no."

The Ponca had lived along the Niobrara for many generations. "We have always been peaceful!" the chief declared. "The land is our own. We do not want to part with it. I have broken no treaties. The president has no right to take the land from me."

But Mr. Kemble said the tribe must move.

Standing Bear stood and said, "This is our land; we were born here. We are growing old here. We had hoped to die here."

Mr. Kemble said the decision had been made. "When the president says something, it must be done."

The Ponca chiefs finally agreed to visit the new place. Standing Bear said, "If we do not like the land, we can tell the president so. If we do like it, we can tell the president so."

Mr. Kemble told the government what the chiefs said. The government sent back a message. It said the chiefs could come to see "the Great Father"—the president of the United States—only if they agreed to move to the new home.

The Ponca chiefs did not understand. The men who interpreted the English words for the Ponca did not make clear what was to happen.

The chiefs talked together. They said, "There can be no harm in going down and seeing the land. If we do not like it, we will not take it."

On February 2, 1877, Mr. Kemble took the chiefs by wagon to Yankton in Dakota Territory. There they received new clothes like the ones the white men wore. Then they got on a train to Kansas. From there they rode in wagons to Oklahoma.

Along the way they stopped at the Osage Reservation. This tribe was related to the Ponca. They were very poor. They told the

Ponca that the land there was bad.

Mr. Kemble took the chiefs all over Indian Territory. He told them to pick out the best place. But they did not like the dry country. It was full of rocks. It was not good farmland.

The inspector took the chiefs to a hotel in Arkansas City. The chiefs were unhappy. They told Kemble they did not like the land. They wanted to go to Washington DC, and talk to President Hayes. Mr. Kemble said they had to choose new land before they could see the president. He also told them they had to give up their old land.

The chiefs said no. They wanted to go home. Mr. Kemble refused to pay for the train trip back to Nebraska. So the chiefs decided to walk.

They headed north one cold February day. They had very little money. They sold some tomahawks and peace pipes and had eight dollars. They also tried to sell their moccasins to buy tickets. But all the railroad agents had been warned not to let the chiefs on a train. Now the chiefs knew they would be arrested if they were caught. They stayed away from towns.

Their moccasins wore out. They walked barefoot over the open prairie. They ate corn they found in fields. They found shelter in haystacks, or they slept on the hard ground. After fifty days they came to the Otoe Reservation in southern Nebraska. There they had food, and they rested. They got new moccasins. They were given horses to finish their trip home.

In late March they came to the Omaha Reservation. Many were sick, and all were hungry. The Omaha fed them and let them rest. The chiefs sent a telegram to President Hayes. They told the president about the bad

way they had been treated. But they got no answer.

The chiefs went back to their village, but Inspector Kemble was there by then. He had orders to move all the Ponca to Indian Territory.

5

The Move

"You must move or the soldiers will shoot you," Inspector Kemble ordered the Ponca. When they refused, he said they would be given no food or supplies.

In the middle of April 1877, some of the tribe members started south. They wanted to go. Still Standing Bear and his followers refused to move. He and his brother Big Snake were arrested. They were put in jail at Fort Randall in Dakota Territory. The commander of the fort was sorry for the Ponca. He asked President Hayes to cancel the move to Indian Territory. But the president did not answer.

Standing Bear and Big Snake were sent back to their village. They and the other men were ordered to take everything they owned to the Agency.

The women and children cried in fear. Some of the men wept too. No one wanted to leave. Armed guards watched them, so no one could run away.

On May 16, 1877, Standing Bear and his band of Ponca began the move south. It was raining. The Niobrara River was full and flowing fast. The heavy wagons sank in the mud. The people had to unload them. The men got into the water. They carried every-thing across the river. Then they led the horses and wagons to the other side.

It was cold and wet work. Army troopers on horses guarded the people. Some of the soldiers were swept away by the rushing water. Some Ponca men dove into the cold river to save them.

It was a bad start to a terrible trip. That long march to Oklahoma was called the "Ponca Trail of Tears." The name came from the Cherokee tribe's long "Trail of Tears" walk in 1838. They, like the Ponca, had been forced to move to Indian Territory. Four thousand Cherokee died on that trip.

The Ponca traveled through snow, rain, thunderstorms, and tornados. They were miserable. Many people got sick. Nine Ponca died on their way to Oklahoma. On the second day of the trip a child died. Several

days later a baby named White Buffalo Girl died. This was near Neligh, Nebraska. The white people there buried her in the town's cemetery. Her parents, Black Elk and Moon Hawk, thanked the white people for taking care of their daughter. The people of Neligh have cared for the baby's grave for over one hundred years.

The Ponca had to keep going. They arrived at Milford, Nebraska. There Standing Bear's daughter Prairie Flower died. He and his family wept for the loss.

But there was more sadness to come. After they buried Prairie Flower, the Ponca camped outside of the town. A terrible wind and rainstorm tore through the camp. Several Ponca were hurt, and Standing Bear's baby granddaughter was killed.

The Ponca walked on. On May 29 they came close to Columbus, Nebraska. There they met some members of the Omaha tribe who were waiting for them. One of them was the chief, Iron Eye. He was also known as Joseph La Flesche. His brother White Swan was one of the Ponca chiefs being moved to Indian Territory.

Iron Eye also brought his daughter Susette La Flesche. Her Omaha name was Inshta-theamba, Bright Eyes. She and her father camped with the Ponca. They listened to the sad story of the hard trip. But the Ponca had to go on. Many cried when they said good-bye to the Omaha.

The terrible march of six hundred miles lasted fifty days. At last the Poncas reached Indian Territory. But their hardship did not end.

They had no place to plant crops. They were hungry. The Ponca were also used to the cool climate of the Niobrara and suffered in the wet warmth of Oklahoma. The people and animals were miserable from mosquitoes and bites from bugs they hadn't known up north. They began to get sick from the heat and from a disease called malaria. Many died.

Standing Bear and the other chiefs were now told that they could visit "the Great Father," the president. The chiefs went to Washington DC. They told President Hayes of the Poncas' troubles. But their visit did no good. President Hayes told them they had to go back to Indian Territory.

Life did not get better in Oklahoma. Many more Ponca died.

Standing Bear and his group moved to a new place. There, two rivers flowed together. It reminded them a little of home. The land was also better. But they arrived too late to plant crops, so they had to get food from the government. They also had to live in tents.

Forty-five more Ponca died. Standing Bear was sad that he could do nothing to help his people. His son, Bear Shield, became sick. The boy knew he was dying. He asked his father to bury him back on the Niobrara homeland.

Standing Bear went to see his brother, Big Snake. He told him that he was going to take Bear Shield's body home. He asked Big Snake to watch over the clan. Big Snake helped his brother put the boy's body into a trunk in the bed of an old wagon. Beside it was a teepee and poles for camping on the way.

Standing Bear, eight men, and twenty-one women and children left Indian Territory on January 2, 1879. They had very little food and not much money. They moved north over the frozen plains. Kind white settlers helped them on the way. Finally, after sixty-two days, they arrived in Nebraska. They camped near the Omaha Reservation.

Standing Bear and his band had survived another long journey. Chief Iron Eye of the Omaha and his daughter Susette welcomed them. The Omaha gave the Ponca food and places to rest. But there was more trouble ahead for Standing Bear and his people.

Friends

The U.S. government ruled that an Indian had to get permission to leave a reservation. Standing Bear and his followers left Oklahoma without such permission.

"I stayed till one hundred and fifty-eight of my people had died," Standing Bear explained. "Then I ran away with thirty of my people, men and women and children. Some of the children were orphans."

The government wanted Standing Bear and his band punished for leaving the reservation without permission. On March 27, 1879, General George Crook of Fort Omaha sent his soldiers to arrest them. Crook had orders to return the Ponca to Indian Territory.

General Crook was a famous Indian fighter who was sorry for the tribes he had to fight. He studied their languages and their customs to understand them better. He was unhappy about having to do what he called his "disagreeable duty," but he had to follow orders.

The commander of the fort, Colonel John H. King, also felt sorry for the Ponca. He reported that the band was too sick to move and the horses were too weak to travel.

The Omaha were upset at the arrest of the

Ponca. They called them "our brothers and sisters, our uncles and our cousins." They gave the Ponca some land to grow crops. Chief Iron Eye and his daughter Susette wanted to help the Ponca even more.

Iron Eye had come to realize that if Indians wanted to survive, they would have to live like white men. They would need to speak and write English. For that reason he had sent his own children to the church boarding school on the Omaha Reservation. Susette had also gone to a private school for girls in New Jersey.

After Susette graduated, she returned to the Omaha Reservation to help her people. She spoke and wrote English very well. She became a teacher at an Omaha Reservation school and later she became a principal there.

Susette and her father went to see General Crook. They told him the sad story of the Poncas' trip to Indian Territory. They told

him about the many deaths on the trail and the problems in Oklahoma. They asked the general to let Standing Bear and his band stay in Nebraska. It was late at night when Susette and her father left.

General Crook thought about what to do. Early the next morning, March 30, 1879, he went to the *Omaha Daily Herald*. He spoke with Thomas Henry Tibbles, an editor of the newspaper.

Susette also met with Tibbles. She understood the white men's ways. She wanted them to know how badly the Ponca had been treated. She hoped they would feel sorry for the band and try to help. As a newspaper man, Tibbles could write the stories for the nation to read.

Thomas Henry Tibbles had spent many years among Indian tribes. He understood them. He wanted to interview Standing Bear. At first Standing Bear did not want to talk to the white man. Then Tibbles gave some of the secret signs of the Soldier Lodge Society, a special band. Years before he had been allowed to join it. He knew Standing Bear was also a member. The chief recognized the signs and spoke with Tibbles.

At Fort Omaha General Crook also interviewed Standing Bear. Standing Bear told him that he was sad Bear Shield had died. The boy had been learning to read and write so that he could help his father get along with the whites. The chief also told the general how unhappy he was that so many Ponca had died in Oklahoma.

General Crook felt sorry for Standing Bear. But he had to obey orders and arrest Standing Bear to stand trial. He would let the band rest at Fort Omaha. He gave them food so they could be strong enough to return to Oklahoma.

The churches of Omaha also helped Standing Bear. They formed the Omaha Ponca Relief Committee. They sent letters to Washington DC. They asked that the Ponca be allowed to stay in their homeland or with the Omaha.

Henry Tibbles wrote newspaper stories that helped Standing Bear's cause. But he knew that more had to be done to help the chief. General Crook told him about a U.S. law called *habeas corpus*. Tibbles thought it would be a good idea to use the law to help the chief.

The words are Latin, and they mean "you have the body" of the law on your side. It is a way to make sure a person is not wrongly put in prison. Tibbles believed that Standing Bear should be protected under the U.S. laws. This was the first time an Indian would claim to have the same rights as any other person in the United States.

7

The Trial

Before the trial U.S. Indian Commissioner Ezra Hayt said that Standing Bear was a troublemaker. He also reported that the Ponca in Indian Territory were healthy and doing well there.

Standing Bear said the commissioner was lying. He had a letter that Hayt had sent him in March 1876. In it Hayt wrote that Standing Bear was a reliable Indian. Hayt's letter also said Standing Bear had set a good example for the other Ponca.

An army lieutenant said the chief was quiet, well behaved, and a friend to the white people. But these good reports did not help Standing Bear. He would still have to go to trial.

The case was called "Standing Bear vs. Crook." General George Crook had agreed to be named as an agent of the U.S. government. He had ordered the soldiers to arrest the Ponca.

The trial was held in Omaha on May 1, 1879. Susette LaFlesche interpreted for Standing Bear. She spoke in Ponca to him. She told him what was being said in English. Then she changed his Indian words to

English so that the court could understand the chief.

This was a historic trial. It was the first time an Indian had been in the Omaha courtroom. The room was packed. Newsmen came to write stories for the nation to read. Lawyers and judges wanted to know how the law would work. Ministers, church members, and many other white people came. They were all curious to know what would happen.

Henry Tibbles found two lawyers, John Webster and Andrew Poppleton. They agreed to help without asking for money.

The lawyers had to show that Standing Bear had been living like a law-abiding white man. He was a farmer, and he had sent his children to school. Webster said the Ponca were not "savages or wanderers." Because they lived like the whites, they should be protected by the law.

Genio Lambertson was the lawyer for the United States. He said that Indians were not American citizens. They had no rights under the U.S. Constitution. Lambertson claimed that Standing Bear could not sue General Crook.

Standing Bear was allowed to speak. He was a tall, dignified man. Over his shoulders he wore a red blanket. An eagle feather was tied in his long hair. He wore a necklace of bear claws and a Thomas Jefferson peace medal.

Standing Bear held out his hand. He said, "That hand is not the color of yours, but if I pierce it, I shall feel pain. If you pierce your hand, you also feel pain. The blood that will flow from mine will be the same color as yours. I am a man. The same God made us both."

The crowded courtroom was silent after

Standing Bear's speech. Some of the women cried. General Crook covered his face with his hands. Then people clapped and cheered. The general stood up and shook the chief's hand.

The trial was over. Standing Bear and his band were taken back to Fort Omaha.

On May 12, 1879, Judge Elmer Dundy gave his decision. He ruled that an Indian was a person with the same rights as those of white people. But Standing Bear and his followers were still not free to go home.

8

Home

Standing Bear and his followers had to stay at Fort Omaha. Their old home was still Sioux land. They needed permission to stay on any reservation—or to leave one. They could not even visit their Omaha relatives.

Again Standing Bear did not wait for permission. He went to the Ponca burial place and put Bear Shield's body in the ground. He had kept his promise to bury his son at home. But Standing Bear could not stay there. Other than Fort Omaha, he had no home.

Henry Tibbles thought of a place for the band to live. It was near Decatur, Nebraska, and it was close to the Omaha Reservation.

Many of Standing Bear's people were still sick after the long trip from Oklahoma. They needed to earn money to buy food. Some of the healthier men chopped firewood. They sold the wood to the people in Decatur. Standing Bear and the others went to church. Again they tried to live like the whites.

The Omaha Ponca Relief Committee again helped the Ponca as they tried to rebuild their lives.

General Crook studied the maps of

Nebraska and the Dakota Territory. He found some islands in the Niobrara River that were not part of the Sioux Reservation. He helped Standing Bear and his band get permission to use those lands, which were close to their old home.

Standing Bear thanked the men who had helped in the trial. He called Henry Tibbles his brother and gave him some beaded buckskin leggings. Standing Bear shook Tibbles's hand and said, "While there is one Ponca alive, you will never be without a friend."

To John Webster he gave a tomahawk. Standing Bear put it on the floor and said, "I have no more use for it. I have found a better way."

He gave a headdress to Andrew Poppleton. It had once been worn by the chief who had signed the first Ponca treaty with the United States. Standing Bear told the lawyer, "I

thank you for what you have done. I want to get my land back. I wish to live there and be buried with my fathers."

Standing Bear's friends thought of a way to raise money for the Ponca. Henry Tibbles set up a lecture tour for Standing Bear. Susette and her brother, Frank La Flesche, interpreted for him. They visited the eastern cities of the United States.

Many people came to hear Standing Bear. They liked the way he spoke and the way he looked. He was a handsome man who stood straight and tall. He wore his red robe and his bear claw necklace. They called him a dignified warrior.

People also liked Susette. She was quiet and pretty. They called her an Indian princess.

Henry Tibbles took care of all the details of the tour. In October they were in Boston

when Henry got bad news from home. His wife had died. She was buried the morning he got the telegram.

Standing Bear also had sad news. His brother Big Snake was dead. Big Snake had tried to leave Indian Territory, just as Standing Bear had done. The army forced him and his followers back to the reservation. When soldiers came to arrest him, Big Snake said he had done nothing wrong and was not armed. He sat down and refused to move. The soldiers beat him. He stood up and was shot and killed.

Standing Bear was sad that Big Snake was dead. He also felt sorry that Tibbles's wife was gone. But he told his friend that they had to continue the tour for the good of all the Ponca.

They kept on until December 12, when the group went home.

Back on his island home, Standing Bear was pleased to see how well his people were doing. Their friends in Omaha had given them farm tools and wagons. They had crossed the river to plant crops in their old fields.

Standing Bear's white neighbors welcomed him home. They told him they hoped he would get his land back. One year after the trial Judge Dundy ruled that the Ponca still had title to their old homeland.

On March 3, 1881, Congress passed the Ponca Relief Bill. Under the terms of the bill, the Ponca who were still in Indian Territory could return to Nebraska. If they stayed in Oklahoma, they would get only 160 acres of land per man. In Nebraska each man would be given 320 acres. But that land was still part of the Sioux Reservation.

The government invited the Sioux chiefs to a meeting in Washington DC. There they agreed to give the Ponca tribe twenty-five thousand acres of their Niobrara homeland.

The government believed that all reservations should be divided so that each Indian owned his own land. Farmland would be "allotted" or given to individual persons. These were the terms of the Dawes Act of 1887. Any land left over was to be sold to the whites.

Once again the Ponca lived on the good earth of the Niobrara and Missouri Rivers. But because of the Dawes Act, they lost some of their homeland.

In 1890 Standing Bear built a house for his two wives, a baby boy, and three daughters. Two orphaned grandsons also lived with him.

Standing Bear farmed the land that he now legally owned. He was happy to be home. There he died on September 3, 1908.

9

After Standing Bear

The land where Standing Bear lived and died belonged to him. Other people in the tribe also owned farms. This ownership was the result of the Dawes Act of 1887. It was also called the Allotment Act. That act divided the reservation land into farms for individual Indians. Leftover land was opened to white homesteaders. As a result, the Ponca lost more land.

In 1962 Standing Bear's Ponca tribe in Nebraska was in danger again. Fewer and fewer Ponca lived on the old Niobrara homelands. Much of that land had been sold off.

The U.S. government decided not to recognize the Nebraska Ponca Indians, or Northern Ponca, as a tribe. Since they were no longer considered a tribe, the government decided they did not need a reservation. For years after that, the Ponca worked to be accepted again as a Nebraska tribe. Finally in 1990 the government once again recognized the Ponca tribe of Nebraska or the Northern Ponca.

The Ponca of Nebraska are now rebuilding their culture and regaining their lands. Their headquarters and other buildings are at

Niobrara, Nebraska, near their old home-lands. There are also other Ponca tribal buildings in Lincoln, Omaha, and Norfolk, Nebraska, and in Sioux City, Iowa.

As part of this renewal the tribe and the state of Nebraska honor Standing Bear of the Ponca in many ways. In the Nebraska State Capitol Building, there is a Hall of Honor. One of the statues there is of Chief Standing Bear. The statue honors him and his place in Nebraska history.

May 12 is "Chief Standing Bear Day" in Nebraska. Every year at the Standing Bear Breakfast, held in Lincoln or Omaha, his story is celebrated. On the same day the winners of the Standing Bear Scholarship and Essay Contest are recognized.

A bridge across the Missouri River near Niobrara also bears Standing Bear's name. In Omaha the story of the trial is displayed on signs and artwork at the Federal Courthouse. The Crook House at Fort Omaha shows the general's relationship with the chief and his role in Standing Bear's trial.

Oklahoma honors Chief Standing Bear too. In Ponca City, Oklahoma, a tall, standing statue of the chief looks out over the prairies where he began his walk home to Nebraska. A powwow, or special dance celebration, is held in Ponca City every year to honor him as well.

The town of Neligh, Nebraska, never forgot the Ponca's sad journey south. For 134 years the people of the town took care of White Buffalo Girl's grave. On May 22, 2011, the Ponca and Omaha tribes thanked the people of Neligh. They had a ceremony and gave gifts to the elders of the town. They also presented a plaque to the mayor.

Standing Bear led the way for American

Indians to seek justice. But since that famous trial, Indians have had to struggle for these rights over and over again. They continue to work for fairness because of Standing Bear's example.

Standing Bear of the Ponca will never be forgotten.

Timeline

1803

Area now Nebraska is part of U.S. Louisiana Purchase.

1804

Lewis and Clark travel up the Missouri and see Ponca village.

Poncas live at Niobrara.

1817

Ponca sign first treaty with U.S. government. Peace and friendship is promised between the two parties.

1819

U.S. Army establishes Fort Atkinson, Nebraska's first fort.

1823

First permanent white settlement at Bellevue, Nebraska.

1825

Ponca sign second treaty with U.S. government, recognize U.S. rule. In return, tribe is to be protected.

1829

Andrew Jackson is president of the United States.

Standing Bear is born.

1830

Ponca village is regular stop for fur traders. Artists Catlin and Bodmer paint picture of the village.

1833

Ponca no longer live in earthen lodges but in teepees.

1834

Indian Territory is established in Oklahoma.

1840

Thousands of settlers travel across Nebraska on the Oregon Trail.

Thomas Henry Tibbles is born.

1854

Nebraska Territory is organized.

Inshtatheamba, Bright Eyes, Susette La Flesche is born.

1858

Ponca sign third treaty with U.S. government.

1859

Poncas sign fourth treaty with U.S. government. It does not include burial ground or their best farmland.

1860

Abraham Lincoln is elected president.

1861

Civil War begins.

1862

Homestead Act brings new settlers into Nebraska.

1865

Civil War ends.

Ponca sign treaty to correct boundaries set in fourth treaty of 1859.

1867

United States purchases Alaska from Russia.

Nebraska becomes a state.

1868

United States signs treaty with Sioux tribes; the treaty includes Ponca lands.

Lincoln becomes state capital of Nebraska.

Sioux increase raids on Ponca.

1875

Ponca ask to live on the Omaha reservation until the government stops the Sioux raids. Request is ignored.

1876

Custer is defeated at the Little Big Horn.

1877

Rutherford Hayes becomes nineteenth president of the United States.

February 2: Ponca chiefs visit Indian Territory.

February 19: Ponca chiefs walk home from Indian Territory.

November: Ponca chiefs visit President Hayes.

1878

May 16–July 9: Poncas travel by wagon and on foot to Indian Territory.

December: On his deathbed Bear Shield asks to be buried at home in Niobrara.

1879

January 2: Standing Bear and followers leave for Niobrara.

March 4: Standing Bear's group reaches Nebraska.

April 30: The case of *Standing Bear v. Crook* is brought before U.S. district court.

May 12: Judge Elmer S. Dundy rules in favor of Standing Bear.

Government appeals to the U.S. Supreme Court.

Bear Shield's bones are buried.

Tibbles, Standing Bear, and Frank and Susette La Flesche go on lecture tour to raise money for the Ponca and Indian reform.

1880

U. S. Supreme Court dismisses government
appeal of Judge Dundy's ruling.

1881

March 3: U. S. Congress passes Ponca Relief
Bill.

President Garfield is assassinated

In Knox County 26,236 acres are returned to
the Ponca.

1882

Susette La Flesche and Henry Tibbles marry.

1887

U.S. Congress passes the Dawes Act.

1890

General Crook dies.

1903

Susette La Flesche Tibbles dies.

1908

Theodore Roosevelt is president of the
United States.

Standing Bear dies.

1928

Thomas Tibbles dies.

Glossary

agency. Place where U.S. government had offices on an Indian reservation.

allotment. A parcel of land given to each Indian.

amulet. A good luck item.

ceremony. A way of conducting a special event or service.

clan. Many related families.

commissioner. An officer of the United States.

cradleboard. A baby carrier.

elder. A respected older person.

lecture. A talk to teach something about a topic.

Ma-ch-nah-zha. "Standing Bear" in the Ponca language.

malaria. A disease caused by the bite of a mosquito.

reservation. An area of land where American Indians had to live.

sacred. Holy.

smallpox. A disease in which a person developed a high fever and bad pimples that burst and left little pit (pox) marks in the skin. Many Indians died from the illness.

Soldier Lodge Society. A group like a club to which only brave men could belong. They had to do the Sun Dance.

Sun Dance. A dance held in the summer. Indian men moved in a circle while looking at the sun. They had no food or water for four days. If a man finished the dance, he could become a member of the Soldier Lodge Society.

territory. A large area of land. Nebraska was called a territory before it became a state.

Thunderbird. The name for an eagle.

treaty. An agreement between two or more groups such as tribes and governments.

umbilical cord. A string-like tether that connects a baby to its mother before it is born. After a baby's birth, Indians saved it.

They believed it would give them good luck.

Vision Quest. A ritual in which boys in their early teens would go off on their own with no food or water for four days. They would have a dream or vision that would give them special power.

Wakanda (wah-kahn-dah). The Ponca name for the Great Spirit or God.

Suggested Reading

Bolton, Jonathan W., and Claire M. Wilson. "La Flesche, Susette." In *Scholars, Writers and Professionals, American Indian Lives*. New York: Facts on File, 1995. American Indian History Online. Facts on File. http://www.fofweb.com/activelink2.asp?ItemID=WE43&iPine=ind0051&SingleRecord=True (accessed January 3, 2008).

Crook, George. *General George Crook: His Autobiography*. Norman: University of Oklahoma Press, 1986.

Dando-Collins, Stephen. *Standing Bear Is a Person: The True Story of a Native American's Quest for Justice*. Cambridge MA: Da Capo, 2005.

Dorsey, James Owen. *The Cegiha Language*. Washington DC: Government Printing Office, 1890.

———. *Omaha and Ponka Letters*. Washington DC: Government Printing Office, 1891.

———. *Omaha Sociology*. Third Annual Report of the U. S. Bureau of Ethnology to the Secretary of the Smithsonian Institution, 1881–82. New York: Johnson Reprint Corporation, 1970.

Kidd Green, Norma. *Iron Eye's Family*. Lincoln: Nebraska State Historical Society, 1996.

Mathes, Valerie Shere, and Richard Lowitt. *The Standing Bear Controversy: Prelude to Indian Reform*. Urbana: University of Illinois Press, 2003.

"Ponca." *Indians of Nebraska*. Lincoln: Nebraska Indian Commission, n.d.

Ponca Tribe of Nebraska. *Ponca Tribe of Nebraska*. 2008. http://www.poncatribe-ne.org/about.php.

Sneve, Virginia Driving Hawk. *The Cherokees*. New York: Holiday House, 1996.

———. *Completing the Circle*. Lincoln: University of Nebraska Press, 1995.

Starita, Joe. *I Am a Man*. New York: St. Martin's Press, 2008.

Tibbles, Thomas Henry. *Standing Bear and the Ponca Chiefs*. Lincoln: University of Nebraska Press, 1995.

The Trial of Standing Bear http://www.nebraskastudies.org/0600/stories/0601_0102.html Facts on File, Inc. American Indian History Online. http://www.fofweb.com/activelink2.asp?ItemID=WE43&iPine=ind6518&SingleRecord=True (accessed January 3, 2008).